INTRODUCTION

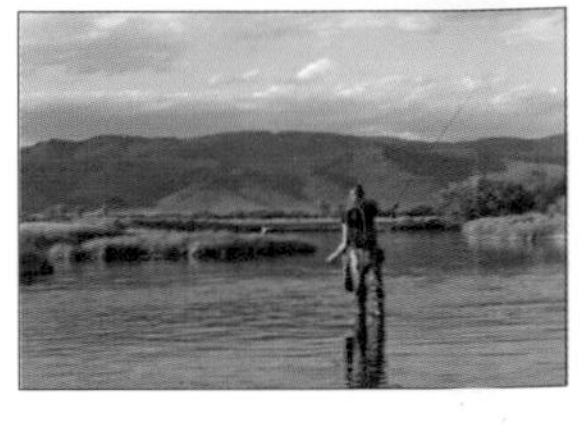

Salmonids are a family of fish revered as some of the most popular and sought-after sport and food fish in the world. The beauty and diversity of the species, and the settings in which they occur attract anglers, naturalists, photographers and artists alike to study and pursue them. Most species live in cold to cool waters throughout the Northern Hemisphere. The main genera include Pacific trout and salmon (*Oncorhynchus*), Atlantic salmon and trout (*Salmo*), char and trout (*Salvelinus*), grayling (*Thymallus*) and freshwater whitefish (*Coregonus*, *Prosopium*, *Stenodus*).

Most salmonids live in fresh water throughout their lives. Some species – including salmon and coastal trout – have young that migrate to sea for a number years before returning to fresh water to spawn in the streams where they were hatched. They range in size from the diminutive 6 in. (15 cm) Apache trout to the enormous Chinook salmon, that can reach 5 ft. (1.5 m) in length and weigh up to 125 lbs. (56 kg).

PARTS OF A SALMONID

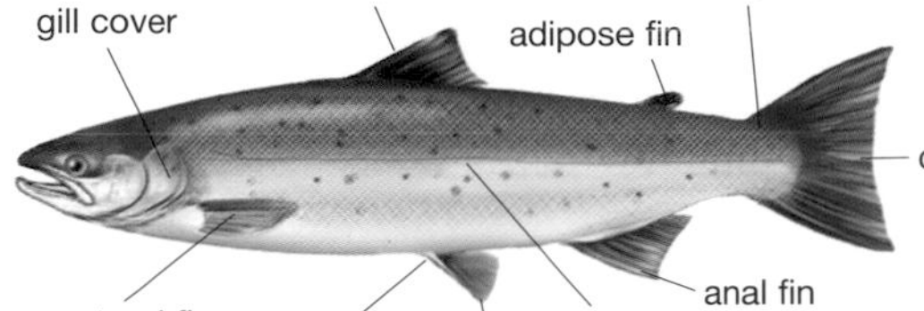

Threats & Conservation

Native populations of trout and salmon are becoming increasingly scarce due to pollution, overfishing, climate change, irrigation diversions and the introduction of non-native fish and other aquatic species including invasive plants. Fortunately, a number of organizations are working to protect and conserve the habitats of native species and contribute hundreds of thousands of volunteer hours each year to restoration projects. Anglers are also becoming more aware of their value as citizen scientists and are forwarding their observations about the condition of habitats they encounter to researchers.

Most illustrations show the adult male in breeding coloration. Colors and markings may be duller or absent during different seasons. The measurements denote the approximate maximum length of species. Illustrations are not to scale.

Made in the USA

Waterford Press publishes reference guides that introduce readers to nature observation, outdoor recreation and survival skills. Product information is featured on the website: **www.waterfordpress.com**

Text & illustrations © 2022 Waterford Press Inc. All rights reserved. To order or for information on custom published products please call 800-434-2555 or email orderdesk@waterfordpress.com. For permissions or to share comments email editor@waterfordpress.com.

ISBN 978-1-62005-423-9
$7.95 U.S.
UPC
10 9 8 7 6 5 4 3 2 1
213501

TROUT & SALMON – An Illustrated Folding Pocket Guide to Familiar Species

Kavanagh/Leung

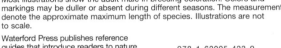

TROUT & SALMON

of North America

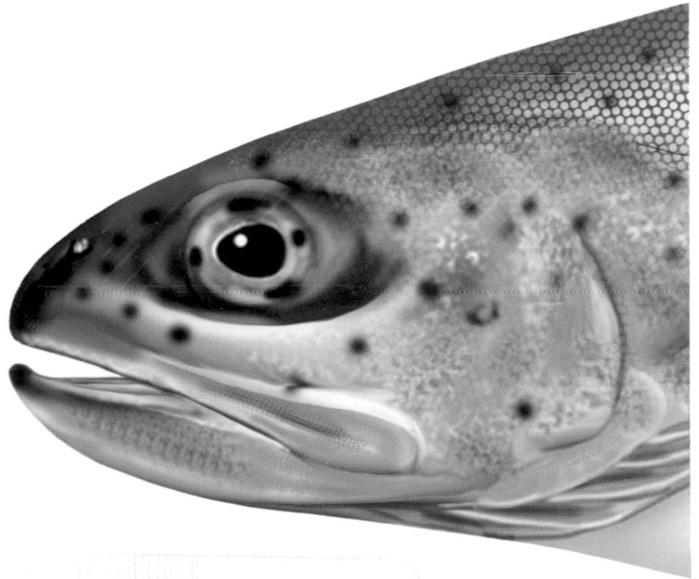

T0124028

An Illustrated Folding Pocket Guide to Familiar Species

PACIFIC TROUT

Rainbow & Redband Trout

The most abundant trout in North America are the rainbow and redband trout. Millions are raised in hatcheries and introduced to lakes and waterways throughout North America.

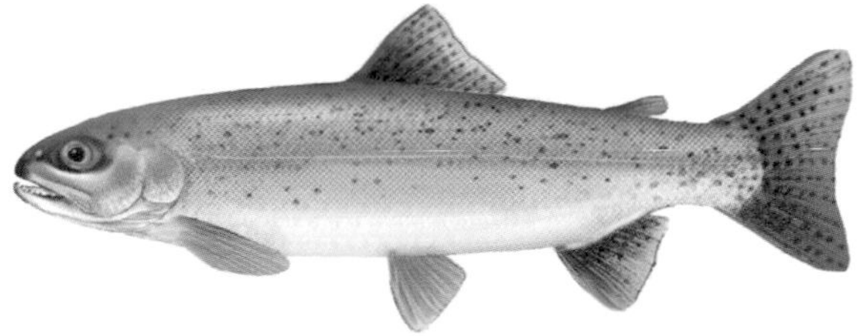

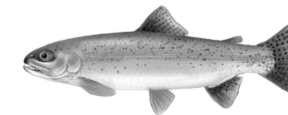

Rainbow Trout *Oncorhynchus mykiss*
Description: Body and fins are dark-spotted. Coloration is highly variable, ranging from steely blue, to yellow-green, to brown. Pink to red side stripe is most vivid in males during breeding season. **Length**: To 44 in. (1.1 m) **Habitat**: Large rivers, lakes and freshwater streams. **Range**: Native to western North America, it has been widely introduced throughout the world. **Comments**: A popular food fish, it is one of the most common farmed fish.

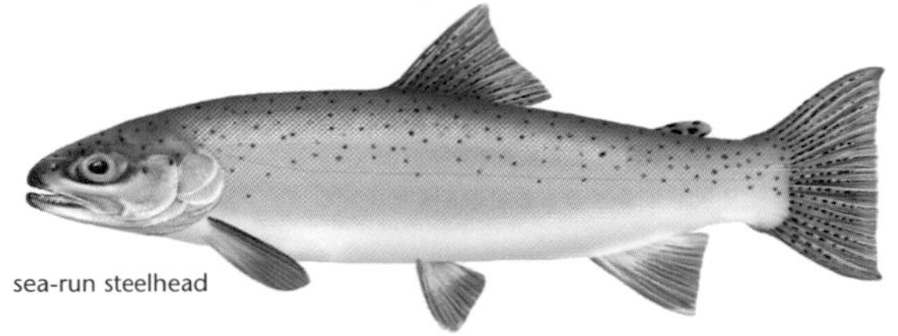

sea-run steelhead

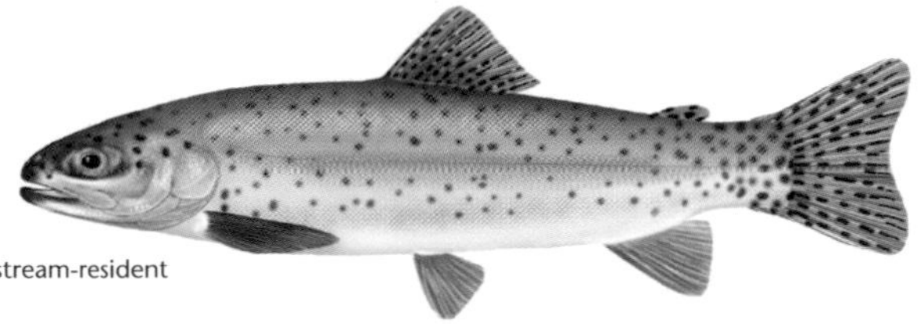

stream-resident

Coastal Rainbow Trout *Oncorhynchus mykiss irideus*
Description: Stream resident is silvery to brassy above, it is heavily spotted on its top, sides and on the dorsal and caudal fin. A bright pink-red stripe runs along the lateral line. **Length**: To 16 in. (40 cm) **Habitat**: Clear, cool streams, lakes and rivers. **Range:** Coastal waters from Aleutian Islands in AK to southern CA. **Comments**: Sea-run steelhead spend 2-3 years at sea before returning to fresh water to spawn. They are silvery with a bluish to greenish back. Side stripe varies from pink to red. They are also much larger than stream residents – to 43 in. (1.1 m).

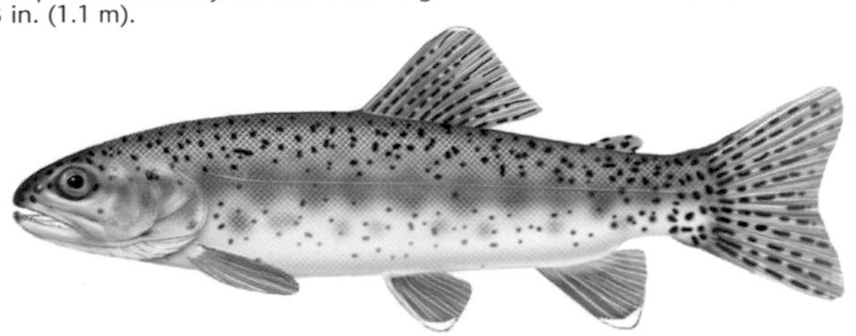

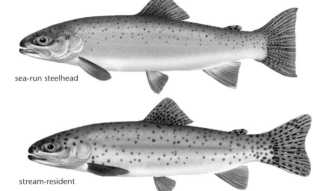

McCloud River Redband Trout
Oncorhynchus mykiss stonei
Description: Yellowish to brownish fish is profusely spotted above the lateral line and has red-rosy gill covers and a pink to red stripe along the lateral line. Pelvic and anal fins are white-tipped. **Length**: To 20 in. (50 cm) **Habitat**: Cool, clear rivers and streams. **Range:** Sacramento River Basin. **Comments**: Two of the native species found in this basin are the McCloud River redband trout (*O.m. stonei*) and the Eagle Lake rainbow trout (*O. m. aquilarium*).

PACIFIC TROUT

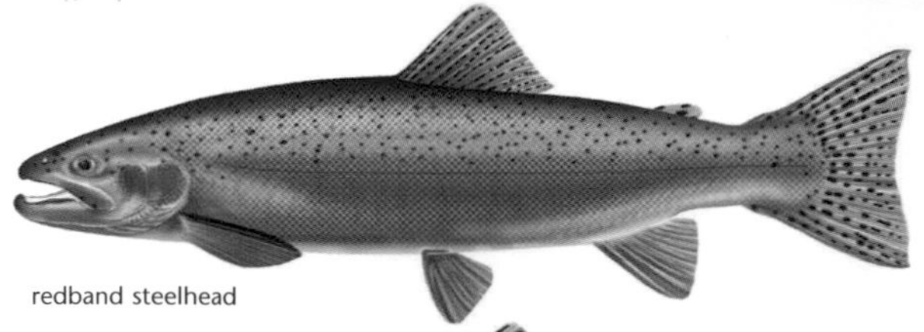

redband steelhead

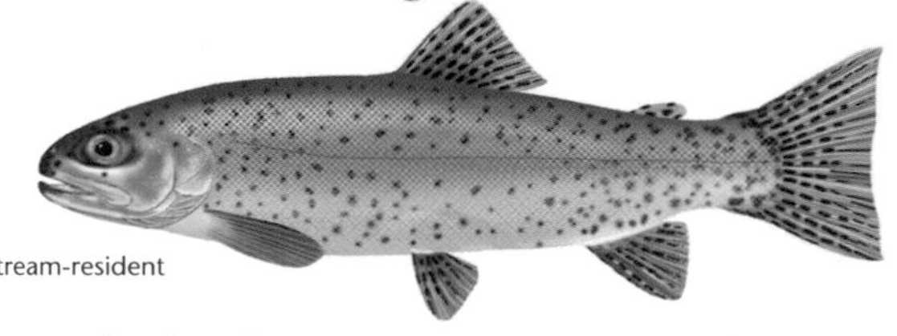

stream-resident

Inland Redband Trout & Redband Steelhead
Oncorhynchus mykiss gairdneri
Description: Stream resident is brassy, orange- and yellow-tinted body is profusely spotted on all but pectoral fin. A rosy stripe runs along the lateral line. **Length**: To 18 in. (45 cm) **Habitat**: Cool streams, rivers and lakes. **Range:** Columbia River and its tributaries. **Comments**: Sea-run redband steelhead spend 2-3 years at sea before returning to fresh water to spawn. Breeding coloration is dark olive with profuse spotting above lateral line and a crimson stripe running from the gill cover down the lateral line and extending to the belly. They are also much larger than stream residents – to 40 in. (1 m).

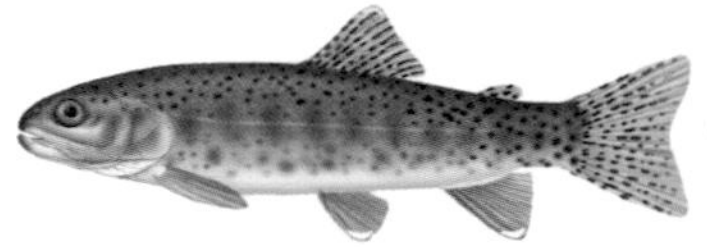

Catlow Basin Redband Trout

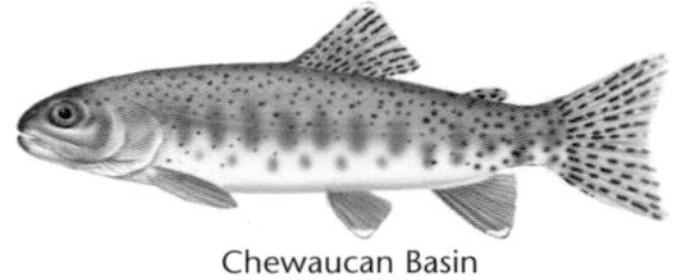

Chewaucan Basin Redband Trout

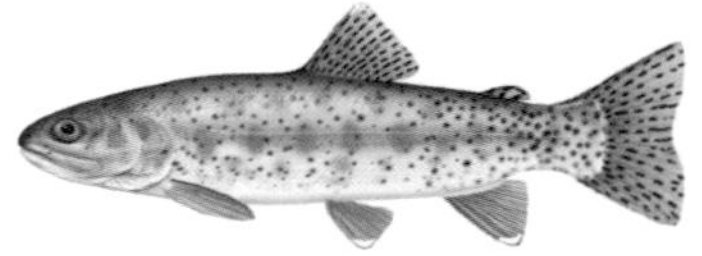

Goose Lake Basin Redband Trout

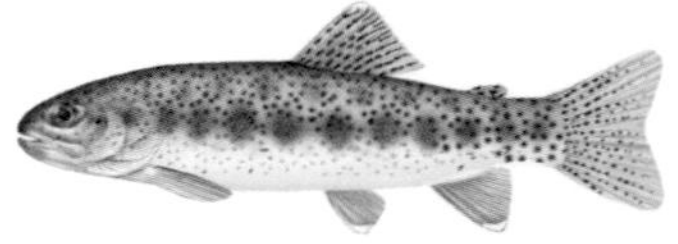

Harney-Malheur Basin Redband Trout

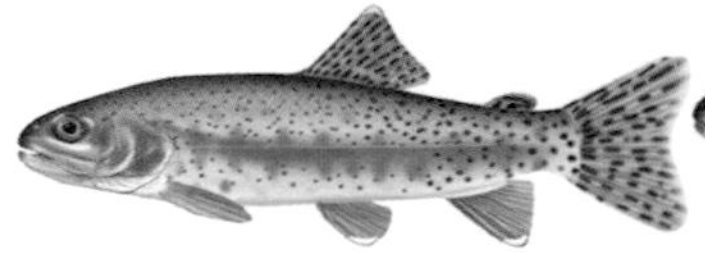

Warner Lakes Basin Redband Trout

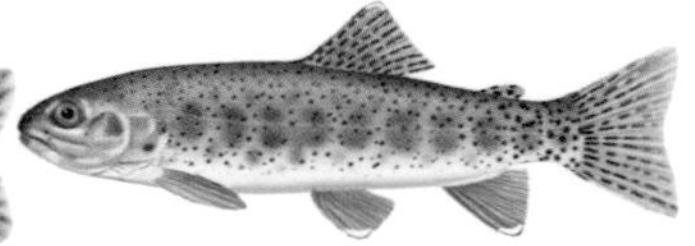

Fort Rock Basin Redband Trout

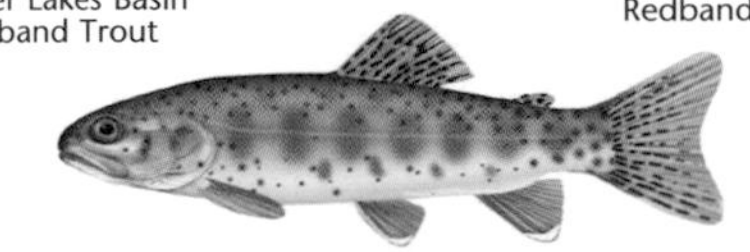

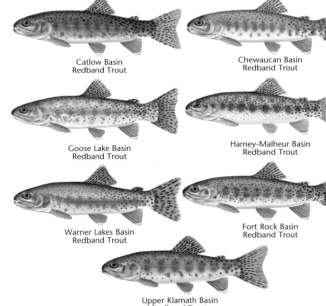

Upper Klamath Basin Redband Trout

Great Basin Redband Trout
Oncorhynchus mykiss newberrii
Great Basin redband trout are native to seven separate isolated basins. Few pure populations have survived due to the introduction of hatchery rainbow trout. **Description**: Most have a rosy to red band along the lateral line, eliptical purplish parr marks on their sides and are heavily spotted. Dorsal, adipose and caudal fins are spotted, the others are not. **Length**: To 20 in. (50 cm) **Habitat**: Rivers and lakes. **Range:** The Northern Great Basin area. **Comments**: Most species are Threatened or Endangered throughout their region.

PACIFIC TROUT

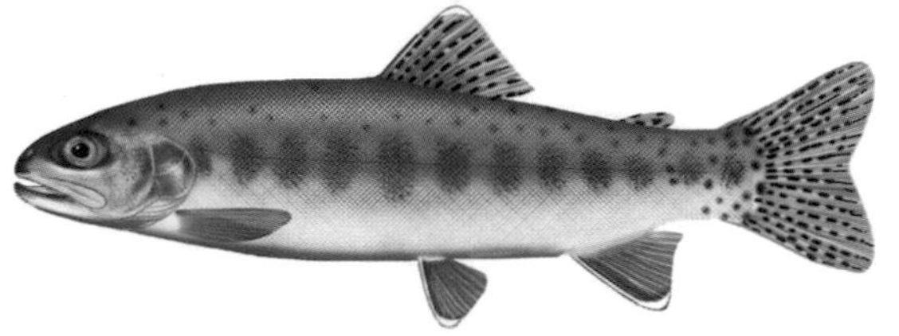

Golden Trout *Oncorhynchus mykiss aguabonita*
Description: Brilliant red-orange fish has golden flanks with red, horizontal bands along the lateral line, several large dark vertical oval marks (known as parr marks) along its sides and large dark spots on its dorsal and caudal fins. **Length**: To 12 in. (30 cm) **Habitat**: Cool lakes and waterways. **Range:** Kern River drainage, CA. **Comments**: Found at elevations from 6,890 feet (2100 m) to 10,000 feet (3000 m).

Gila & Apache Trout

These two subspecies are native to West-central Arizona and East-central New Mexico.

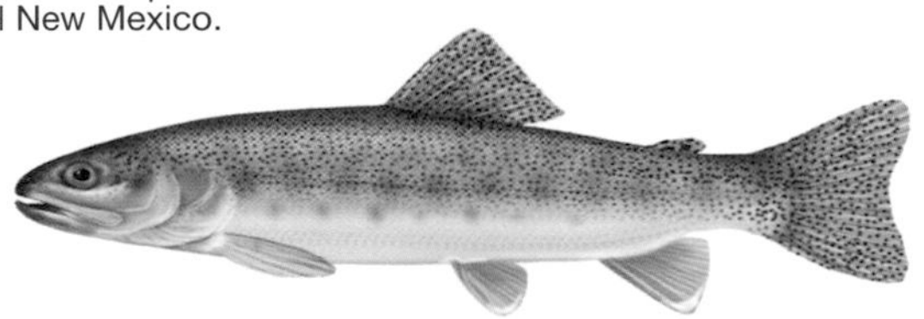

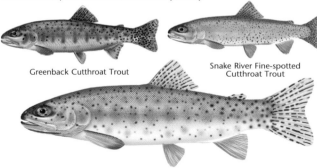

Gila Trout *Oncorhynchus gilae gilae*
Description: Olive to yellow fish has small, irregular black spots on its upper body and on its dorsal and caudal fins. Dorsal, pelvic and anal fins are unspotted. **Length**: To 21 in. (53 cm) **Habitat**: Small, cool streams and creeks. **Range:** Native to the Gila River tributaries. **Comments**: Found above elevations of 6500 ft. (2000 m).

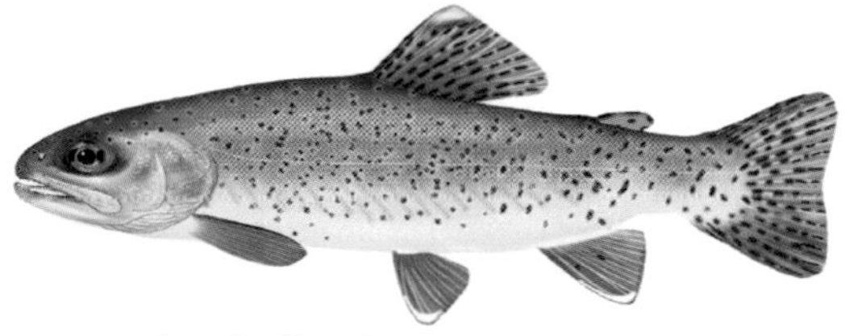

Apache Trout *Oncorhynchus gilae apache*
Description: Has yellow body and fins covered with dark spots on the dorsal side. Dorsal, anal and pelvic fins are white-tipped. **Length**: To 2 ft. (60 cm) **Habitat**: Small, cool streams, stocked in lakes. **Range:** West-central Arizona. **Comments**: Populations are declining owing to the introduction of rainbow trout which hybridize with them.

Cutthroat Trout

There are 14 subspecies of cutthroat trout native to distinct regions that are are believed to be derived from four major lineages – the westslope, coastal, Yellowstone and Lahontan – that diverged from each other about a million years ago. All share the distinctive cutthroat mark of a red-orange slash under the jaw.

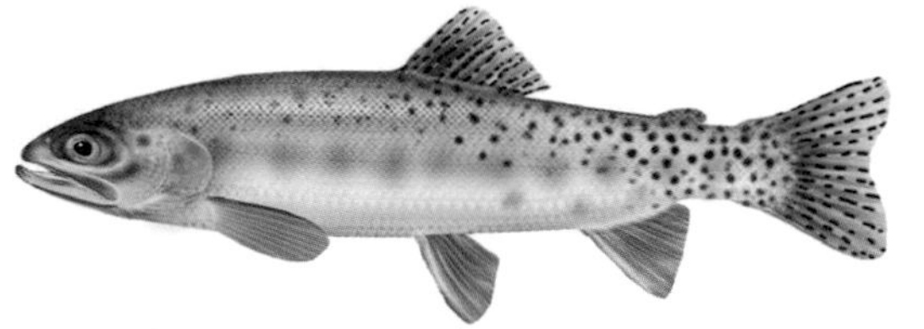

Westslope Cutthroat Trout *Oncorhynchus clarkii lewisi*
Description: Greenish gold body has dark spots clustered toward the tail. Gill covers are purple-blue. **Length**: To 18 in. (45 cm) **Habitat**: Small streams and lakes. **Range:** Native to ID, MT, WA, OR, AB and BC. **Comments**: Remaining populations survive in isolated areas.

PACIFIC TROUT

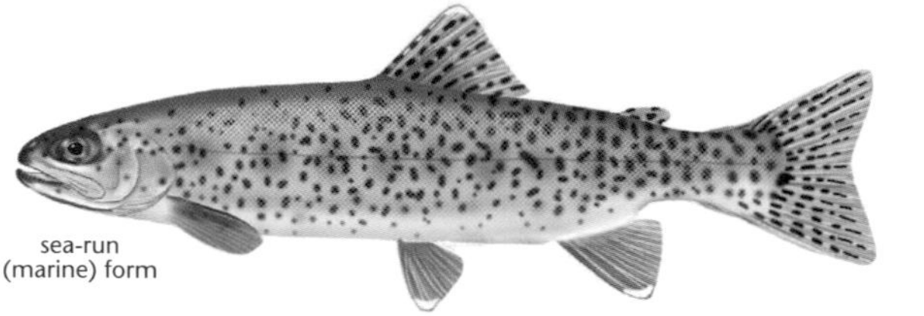

sea-run (marine) form

Coastal Cutthroat Trout *Oncorhynchus clarkii clarkii*
Description: Marine form has a silvery body with a bluish back and is heavily spotted. Cutthroat mark is orangish. Freshwater forms are greenish above and silvery below with pinkish gill covers. **Length**: To 22 in. (55 cm) **Habitat**: Freshwater form found in larger streams and lakes, marine form in nearshore intertidal areas. Range: AK to northern CA. **Comments**: Also called speckled trout (freshwater form) and blueback trout (marine form).

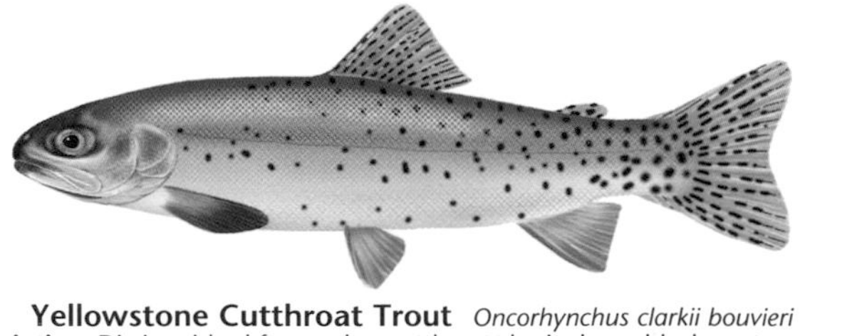

Yellowstone Cutthroat Trout *Oncorhynchus clarkii bouvieri*
Description: Distinguished from other cutthroats by its large black spots clustered toward the tail. Body color is variable, ranging from gray and gold to copper. **Length**: To 2 ft. (60 cm) **Habitat**: Cool streams, rivers and lakes. **Range:** Native to Yellowstone area and northern Rocky Mountain states. **Comments**: Subspecies include Snake River fine-spotted, Greenback, Bonneville, Colorado River, Rio Grande and Yellowfin (extinct).

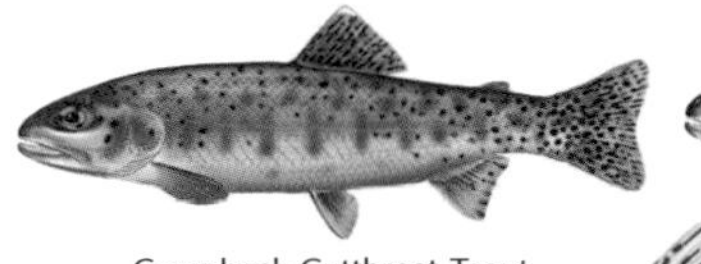

Greenback Cutthroat Trout

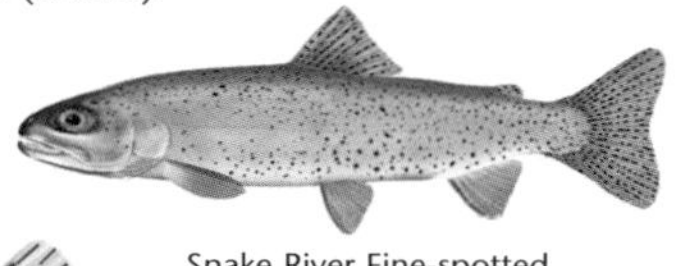

Snake River Fine-spotted Cutthroat Trout

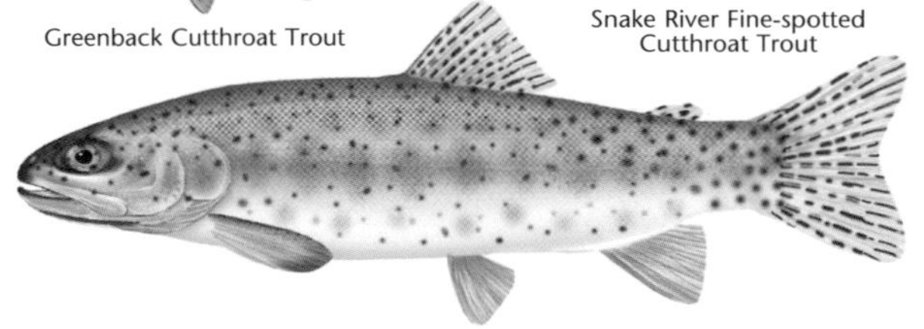

Lahontan Cutthroat Trout *Oncorhynchus clarkii henshawi*
Description: Dorsal side is green-bronze, sides are yellowish with rosy tints along the lateral line. Back, sides and dorsal, adipose and caudal fins are black-spotted. **Length**: To 39 in. (98 cm) **Habitat**: Streams, rivers, ponds and lakes. **Range:** Native to NW Nevada and small sections of CA and UT, it has been introduced elsewhere in the west. **Comments**: Subspecies include Whitehorse Basin, Paiute, Humboldt and Alvord (extinct as a result of hybridization).

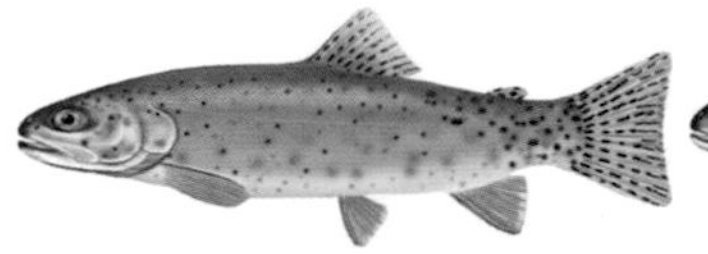

Whitehorse Basin Cutthroat Trout

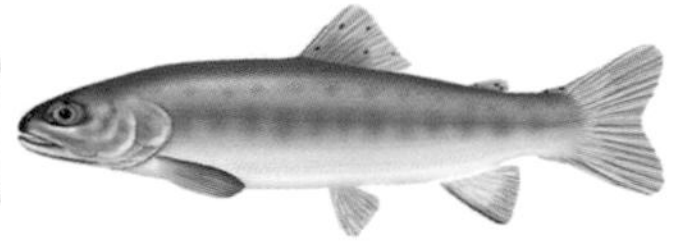

Paiute Cutthroat Trout

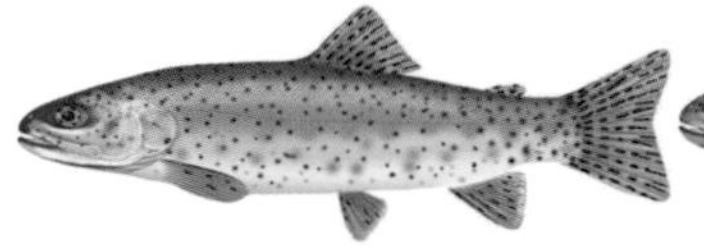

Humboldt Cutthroat Trout

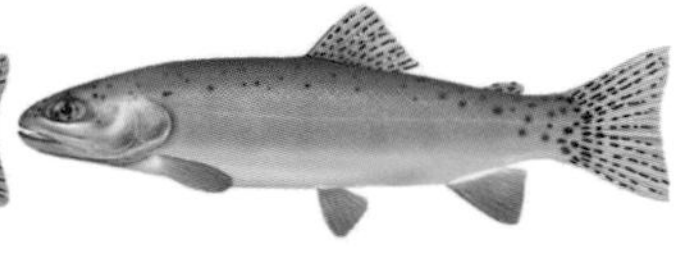

Alvord Cutthroat Trout

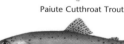

CHAR SPECIES

This group of circumpolar fishes are covered with light spots (cream, pink or red) over a darker body. The pectoral, pelvic and anal fins, and the lower lobe of the tail fin, have a light-colored leading edge.

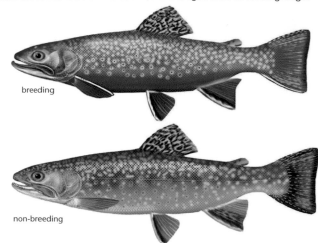

breeding

non-breeding

Brook Trout *Salvelinus fontinalis*
Description: Has wavy yellow marks on dorsal side and dorsal fin. Reddish side spots have blue halos. The breeding male is brilliant red-orange below and has a black belly. **Length:** To 28 in. (70 cm) **Habitat:** Cool, clean rivers and lakes. **Range:** Native to Eastern Canada and Great Lakes south to GA, introduced elsewhere. **Comments:** Hybrids of brook and lake trout – called splake – are a popular sport fish in some areas.

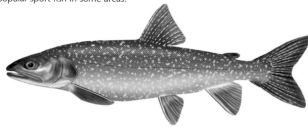

Lake Trout *Salvelinus namaycush*
Description: Blue-gray to olive above, its body is covered in pale, irregular spots. Pelvic, pectoral and anal fins are sometimes red-orange with a white leading edge. Caudal fin is deeply forked. **Length:** To 50 in. (1.25 m) **Habitat:** Deep, cold lakes and rivers. **Range:** AK and most of Canada south to the Great Lakes; introduced elsewhere. **Comments:** The largest North American trout is a prized food fish. Also called mackinaw, lake char and siscowet.

Arctic Char *Salvelinus alpinus*
Description: Coloration and size varies the many different life histories of this species. Color varies from dull gray to lake resident populations to brilliant red for sea-run populations. Has pink to red spots on its back and sides. Caudal fin is slightly forked with a yellowish border. **Length:** To 40 in. (1 m) **Habitat:** Large rivers and lakes. **Range:** Circumpolar, south to New England in east. **Comments:** Occurs further north than any other freshwater fish.

CHAR SPECIES

breeding

non-breeding

Bull Trout *Salvelinus confluentus*
Description: Color ranges from gray to green, back and sides are covered with pale yellowish to reddish spots. Similar to Dolly Varden but has a longer, flatter head. **Length:** To 3 ft. (90 cm) **Habitat:** Cold western rivers and lakes, mountain streams. **Range:** Yukon drainage to Oregon. **Comments:** Lake resident, river resident (including migratory and non-migratory) and sea-run forms occur. A voracious predator.

Dolly Varden *Salvelinus malma*
Description: Green to brown above, its back and sides are covered with small red to yellow spots. Breeding male is green-black above and bright red below. **Length:** To 25 in. (63 cm) **Habitat:** Deep rivers and lakes, nearshore marine waters. **Range:** Western waters from northern AK to Puget Sound, WA. **Comments:** Tend to have a more rounded body than a bull trout.

GRAYLING

Distinguished by their large scales, small mouths and large, sail-like dorsal fins.

Arctic Grayling *Thymallus arcticus*
Description: Dark blue-gray above, it is distinguished by its huge, sail-like, spotted dorsal fin and forked tail. Mouth is small. **Length:** To 30 in. (75 cm) **Habitat:** Clear, cold rivers and lakes. **Range:** Native to Arctic and northern Pacific drainages and the upper Missouri River basin, it has been widely introduced elsewhere. Extinct in the Great Lakes. **Comments:** Spawns in spring in shallow rivers and streams.

BROWN TROUT & ATLANTIC SALMON

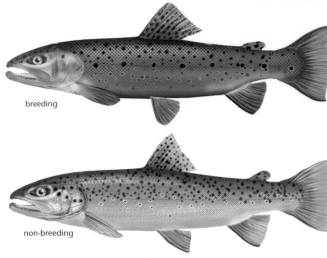

breeding

non-breeding

Brown Trout *Salmo trutta*
Description: Olive to brown above, it is covered with red, black or orange spots, often with white halos. Caudal fin is straight-edged. Breeding male has a hooked jaw and is reddish, orangish or yellowish on its sides and belly. They often have red or orange on their adipose fins, a feature unique to this species. **Length:** To 40 in. (1 m) **Habitat:** Cool, fast-flowing streams and lakes. Some sea-run populations occur in nearshore waters. **Range:** Native to Europe, widely stocked throughout the U.S. and Canada. **Comments:** Like rainbow and cutthroat trout, there are three basic forms, stream-resident, lake-resident and sea-run (anadromous).

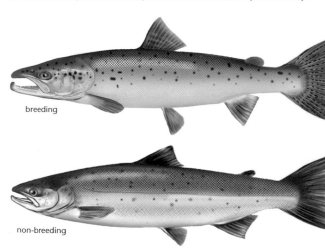

breeding

non-breeding

Atlantic Salmon *Salmo salar*
Description: Has black spots (often X-shaped) on sides (but not on fins) and 2-3 large spots on gill cover. Marine form is silvery. Breeding form is brown-purple on sides and has red spots and an upward hooked lower jaw. **Length:** To 4.5 ft. (1.4 m) **Habitat:** Coastal waters, freshwater lakes and streams. **Range:** Native from Arctic Circle through Quebec to Connecticut River. Many landlocked populations are found in New England and eastern Canada. **Comments:** Unlike Pacific salmon, it does not die after spawning and returns to the sea. The most common commercially farmed salmon.

PACIFIC SALMON

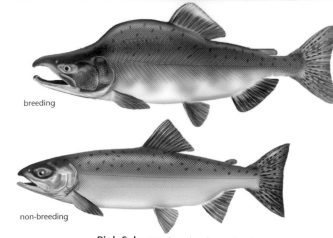

breeding

non-breeding

Coho Salmon *Oncorhynchus kisutch*
Description: Has dark spots on its back and the upper lobe of its caudal fin. Mouth is black and gums are white. Breeding male has red side stripes. **Length:** To 40 in. (1 m) **Habitat:** Shallow to mid-level ocean waters. Returns to coastal streams to spawn, often far inland. **Range:** Bering Strait to central CA. Widely introduced. **Comments:** Also called silver salmon.

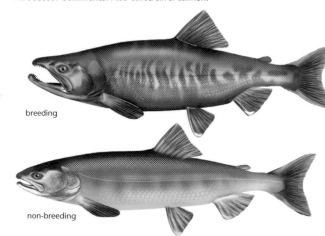

breeding

non-breeding

Chum Salmon *Oncorhynchus keta*
Description: Anal fin and pelvic fins are white-tipped. Breeding male has blotchy red marks along green sides. **Length:** To 44 in. (1.1 m) **Habitat:** Coastal waters, spawns in freshwater streams. **Range:** Arctic Alaska to central CA. **Comments:** Also called dog salmon, they have the largest natural range of all the Pacific salmon.

World Record Trout on All Tackle

Arctic Char	32 lbs. 9 oz.	(14.77 kg)	NT, Canada
Arctic Grayling	5 lbs. 15 oz.	(2.69 kg)	NT, Canada
Apache Trout	5 lbs. 3 oz.	(2.36 kg)	AZ, USA
Brook Trout	14 lbs. 8 oz.	(6.57 kg)	ON, Canada
Brown Trout	44 lbs. 0 oz.	(20.10 kg)	New Zealand
Bull Trout	32 lbs. 0 oz.	(14.51 kg)	ID, USA
Cutthroat Trout	41 lbs. 0 oz.	(18.59 kg)	NV, USA
Dolly Varden	20 lbs. 14 oz.	(9.46 kg)	AK, USA
Gila Trout	3 lbs. 7 oz.	(1.56 kg)	AZ, USA
Golden Trout	11 lbs. 0 oz.	(4.98 kg)	WY, USA
Lake Trout	72 lbs. 0 oz.	(32.65 kg)	NT, Canada
Rainbow Trout	48 lbs. 0 oz.	(21.77 kg)	SK, Canada
			Source: International Game Fish Association (IGFA)

PACIFIC SALMON

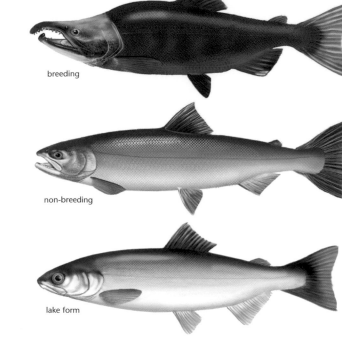

breeding

non-breeding

Pink Salmon *Oncorhynchus gorbuscha*
Description: Has large oval spots on its back and caudal fins. Breeding male has a prominently humped back and pink side stripe. **Length:** To 30 in. (75 cm) **Habitat:** Coastal waters, spawns in freshwater streams. **Range:** Northern AK to Puget Sound, WA. **Comments:** Named for its pink flesh. Also called humpbacked salmon.

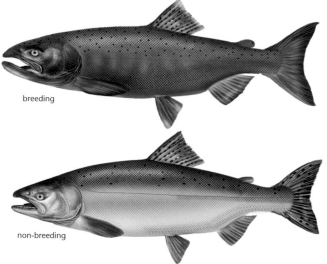

breeding

non-breeding

Chinook Salmon *Oncorhynchus tshawytscha*
Description: Has silvery sides and black spots on its upper body. Gums are black at tooth base. Breeding fish are olive brown to purplish and develop a reddish tint on the belly and tail. **Length:** To 5 ft. (1.5 m) **Habitat:** Shallow to mid-level ocean waters. Returns to large rivers to spawn. **Range:** Bering Strait to central CA. Widely introduced. **Comments:** The largest salmon, it is also called king salmon, tyee, spring salmon and blackmouth.

World Record Salmon on All Tackle

Atlantic Salmon	79 lbs. 2 oz.	(35.89 kg)	Norway
Chinook Salmon	97 lbs. 4 oz.	(44.11 kg)	AK, USA
Chum Salmon	35 lbs. 0 oz.	(15.87 kg)	BC, Canada
Coho Salmon	33 lbs. 4 oz.	(15.08 kg)	NY, USA
Pink Salmon	14 lbs. 13 oz.	(6.74 kg)	WA, USA
Sockeye Salmon	15 lbs. 3 oz.	(6.88 kg)	AK, USA
			Source: International Game Fish Association (IGFA)

PACIFIC SALMON

breeding

non-breeding

lake form

Sockeye Salmon *Oncorhynchus nerka*
Description: Body is lightly speckled and lacks large black spots on back and caudal fins. Marine form is metallic blue-green above and silvery below. Red breeding male has hooked jaws and green head. Tail lacks spotting. **Length:** To 33 in. (83 cm) **Habitat:** Surface ocean waters, spawns in coastal streams. **Range:** Bering Strait to Columbia River WA/OR. Widely stocked. **Comments:** Also called red salmon and blueback salmon. Landlocked lake form called Kokanee salmon do not migrate and may be found in the same lakes as its sea-run relatives. They are able to coexist in the same waters because they eat different foods and spawn in different areas.

FRESHWATER WHITEFISH

Large-scaled fish are distinguished by their compressed body, subterminal mouth and forked caudal fin. Other members of this group include mountain whitefish, round whitefish, pygmy whitefish and cisco.

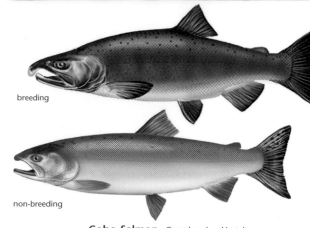

Lake Whitefish *Coregonus clupeaformis*
Description: Brown to blue above, sides are silvery. Note concave forehead. **Length:** To 30 in. (75 cm) **Habitat:** Large rivers and lakes. **Range:** Throughout much of Canada, south to the Great Lakes. **Comments:** Primarily a bottom-feeder, it is a popular table fish. One of the most valuable commercial species in North America.